Alto Saxophone

Level 1

Alfred's
INSTRUMENTAL
EASY
PLAY-ALONG

EASY CHRISTMAS CAROLS
Instrumental Solos

Contents

	Page	Demo	CD Track Play-Along

Arranged by Bill Galliford, Ethan Neuburg and Tod Edmondson

ISBN-10: 0-7390-8395-3
ISBN-13: 978-0-7390-8395-6

Alfred

AWAY IN A MANGER (MEDLEY)

Track 2: Demo
Track 3: Play Along

Music by
JAMES R. MURRAY (1887) and
WILLIAM J. KIRKPATRICK

"Away in a Manger"
Music by JAMES R. MURRAY

Slowly and gently (♩ = 84)

legato

"Away in a Manger (Cradle Song)"
Music by WILLIAM J. KIRKPATRICK

ANGELS WE HAVE HEARD ON HIGH

Track 4: Demo
Track 5: Play Along

Traditional French Melody

Moderately (♩ = 104)

COME, THOU LONG-EXPECTED JESUS

Track 6: Demo
Track 7: Play Along

Music by
ROLAND H. PRICHARD

Gently and flowing (♩ = 112)

GO, TELL IT ON THE MOUNTAIN

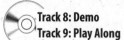
Track 8: Demo
Track 9: Play Along

Traditional Spiritual

Moderately, with a gospel feel (♩ = 104) (♫ = ♪³♪)

molto rit.

WE THREE KINGS

Track 10: Demo
Track 11: Play Along

Moderately slow and tenderly (♩ = 180)
(♩. = 60 This represents the song pulse feel counted in one.)

Words and Music by
JOHN H. HOPKINS, JR. (1857)

IT CAME UPON THE MIDNIGHT CLEAR

Track 12: Demo
Track 13: Play Along

Music by
RICHARD S. WILLIS

HARK! THE HERALD ANGELS SING

Track 14: Demo
Track 15: Play Along

Music by
FELIX MENDELSSOHN

JOY TO THE WORLD

Track 16: Demo
Track 17: Play Along

Music by
GEORGE F. HANDEL

Moderately slow and gentle (♩ = 72)

cresc. poco a poco

O COME, O COME, EMMANUEL

Track 18: Demo
Track 19: Play Along

Music Adapted by
THOMAS HELMORE

Tenderly and flowing (♩ = 120)

rit.　　　　　　　　　　　a tempo　　　rit.

SILENT NIGHT

Track 20: Demo
Track 21: Play Along

Words and Music by
JOSEPH MOHR and FRANZ GRUBER

O COME ALL YE FAITHFUL

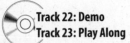

Track 22: Demo
Track 23: Play Along

Music by
JOHN FRANCIS WADE

O LITTLE TOWN OF BETHLEHEM

Track 24: Demo
Track 25: Play Along

Music by
LEWIS H. REDNER

molto rit.

THE FIRST NOEL

Traditional English Carol

Track 28: Demo
Track 29: Play Along

WHAT CHILD IS THIS?

Old English Air

PARTS OF AN ALTO SAXOPHONE AND FINGERING CHART

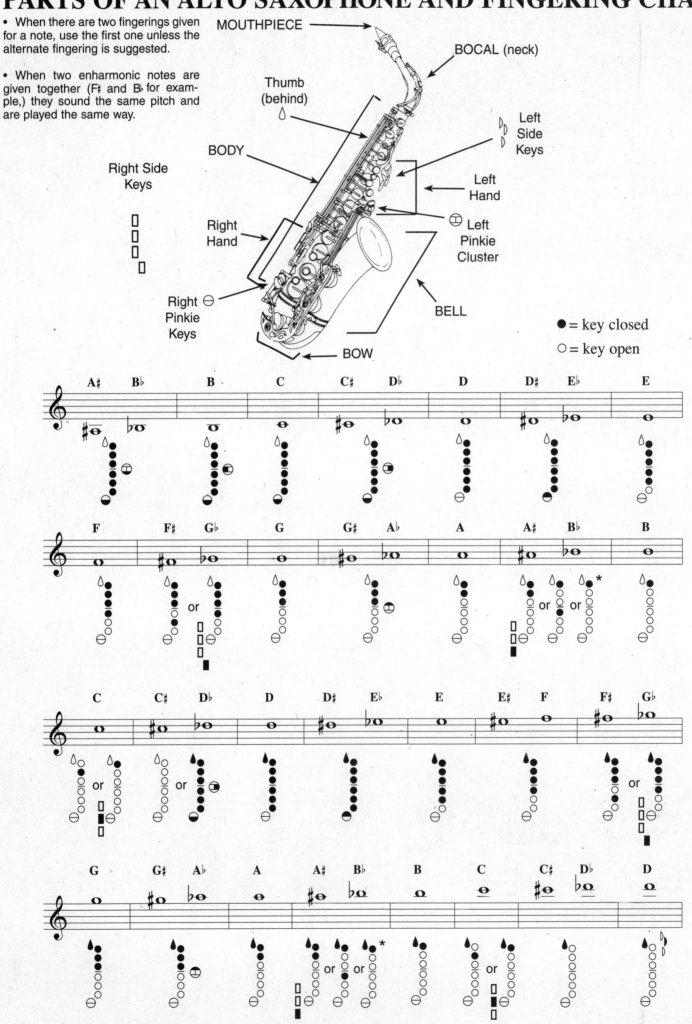

• When there are two fingerings given for a note, use the first one unless the alternate fingering is suggested.

• When two enharmonic notes are given together (F♯ and B♭ for example,) they sound the same pitch and are played the same way.

● = key closed
○ = key open

* Both pearl keys are pressed with the Left Hand 1st finger.